Contents

Any words appearing in the text in bold,
like this, are explained in the Glossary.

The big picture

Computers affect all areas of our lives, yet they have only been around for 50 years. Today, they are amongst our most powerful tools. It has taken vision, luck, and hard work to create systems that work for us in so many ways.

Machines for thinking

For centuries people have wanted tools and machines to take the drudgery out of intellectual as well as physical work. The ancient Chinese invented a simple calculating device, the abacus, thousands of years ago. Now we have tiny computers in hand-held devices that can carry out hugely complicated tasks – and they are so cheap that many people have several.

Pioneer

The first person to try to build a computer was Charles Babbage in the 1820s. In his time, people who needed to do complicated calculations, such as ships' navigators and accountants, looked up printed tables of numbers. These often had mistakes. Babbage designed his Difference Engine and Analytical Engine to compile tables accurately. But as there was no electricity, Babbage's mechanical computers could only use cogs and gears to churn out the results of calculations.

Your mobile phone contains a computer more powerful than the one used to land the Apollo spacecraft on the Moon.

THE CUTTING EDGE

COMPUTERS

Faster, Smaller, and Smarter

Anne Rooney

www.heinemann.co.uk/library
Visit our website to find out more information about **Heinemann Library** books.

To order:
☎ Phone 44 (0) 1865 888066
🗎 Send a fax to 44 (0) 1865 314091
🖳 Visit the Heinemann Bookshop at **www.heinemann.co.uk/library** to browse our catalogue and order online.

First published in Great Britain by Heinemann Library, Halley Court, Jordan Hill, Oxford OX2 8EJ, part of Harcourt Education.
Heinemann is a registered trademark of Harcourt Education Ltd.

Editorial: Sarah Shannon and Kate Bellamy
Design: Richard Parker and Tinstar Design www.tinstar.co.uk
Illustrations: Jeff Edwards
Picture Research: Natalie Gray and Bea Ray
Production: Chloe Bloom

Originated by Digital Imaging
Printed and bound in China by South China Printing Company

ISBN 0 431 13263 1 (hardback)   ISBN 0 431 13269 0 (paperback)
ISBN 978 0 431 13263 1 (hardback)   ISBN 978 0 431 13269 3 (paperback)
10 09 08 07 06   11 10 09 08 07
10 9 8 7 6 5 4 3 2 1   10 9 8 7 6 5 4 3 2 1

British Library Cataloguing in Publication Data
Rooney, Anne
Computers (The Cutting Edge)
004
A full catalogue record for this book is available from the British Library.

Acknowledgements
The publishers would like to thank the following for permission to reproduce photographs:
Dreamworks/Everett/Rex p. 32; Camera press p. 19; Corbis pp. 4, 9, 14, 28, 33, 35, 39, 44, 46; Everett Collections/Rex p. 42; Getty pp. 13, 16, 24, 25; Reuters p. 23; Reuters (Fabrizio Bensch) p. 49; Rex p. 10/11; Rex/Everett p. 34; Rex Features p. 26; Richard Skrenta p. 41; Science & Society Picture Library p. 5; Science Photo Library pp. 8, 31, 36; SipaPress/Rex Features p. 21; SPL pp. 51, 53;

Cover photograph of a girl standing at high tech computer screen, reproduced with permission of Corbis.

Our thanks to Ian Graham for his assistance in the preparation of this book.

Every effort has been made to contact copyright holders of any material reproduced in this book. Any omissions will be rectified in subsequent printings if notice is given to the publishers.

The earliest computers were giants, filling entire rooms. Colossus, destroyed after World War II, has been rebuilt.

Colossus and other giants

One of the first electronic computers was built in England during World War II. It was made at Bletchley Park in Buckinghamshire to break codes the enemy German army was using to pass secret messages. Called Colossus, the computer was so secret that it was destroyed after the war.

Very soon after, ENIAC was built in the United States. Just like Babbage's machine, it was made to compile tables. ENIAC was created by John Mauchly and J. Presper Eckert in 1945/6 to produce firing tables for weapons.

Getting smaller

The first computers were enormous – they could fill an entire room. Even though they were so big, they were not very powerful by modern standards – they could do less computing work than a modern hand-held computer (**PDA**).

It was not until the 1970s that ordinary people could own a computer. Even then, these home computers could not do very much. The first micro- or personal computer was sold as a kit to build at home. It did not have a keyboard, or a screen, and it had no way to store information or instructions. It was very different from the modern personal computers of today.

As computers became smaller, faster, and cheaper, people realized they could use the computers along with other devices. Computers could be used to take readings from equipment and produce meaningful information. They could also be used to turn other equipment on or off to make something happen. This was the beginning of control technology, the use of computers to control other equipment.

Supercomputers

Although the computers most people use now are small, there are still very large computers. Businesses and large organizations like hospitals, governments, and universities have computers that are much more powerful than personal computers. They can also work more quickly. The biggest of these are called **supercomputers**. Supercomputers, like personal computers, can be used for lots of different tasks.

How things change

Computers have improved dramatically as the technologies available to make them have changed. Electronic computers were not possible at all before we had an electricity supply, and only primitive computers could be made before the invention of **transistors**. The development of new electronic parts such as **semiconductors** and **printed circuits**, small-scale engineering, and **microchips** has enabled us to make great advances in computer hardware (the machinery that makes up a computer system).

Just as important are the remarkable people who have imagined new ways of doing things, or who have seen how computers can be used to solve a task or problem. To do anything, a computer has to follow a set of instructions, called a program. If you create a picture or write a document on a computer, you have to use a program to tell the computer what to do.

Computer programs are written in special programming languages that look nothing like ordinary spoken languages.

host kernel: BSM auc
ht@0,f2000000/pci@7/
ting on <dict ID="0"><key>IOPathMatch<
"1">IODeviceTree:/ht@0,f2000000/pci@7/
a/@0:3</string></dict> Jul 4 08:48:58
ervice:/MacRISC4PE/ht@0,f2000000/Apple
C/AppleK2SATARoot/k2-sata@0/AppleK2SAT
ABlockStorageDevice/IOBlockStorageDriv
/IOApplePartitionScheme/Apple_HFS_Un

Writing programs means working out all the stages of a task and converting them into instructions the computer can understand. A program must be easy for people to use so that they can get the computer to do what they want.

Working together

New ideas in computing often come from people wanting to do a task they cannot do on their own, like working out how big the Universe is, or sending a camera inside a pyramid. The people who want to do the task and computer experts work out together exactly what the task involves and how a computer can be made to do it. They may need to make new equipment, such as an especially small robot, or they might need to write a computer program.

Whatever they develop must be tested and improved until it works properly.

Dreaming the future

Our imagination has often been years ahead of our technical capabilities. The dreams of writers and film-makers have inspired people with technical knowledge, who have then worked to turn those dreams into reality.

Everyday computers

There are millions of computers in our homes and cars, and hidden in many common objects. Computers control lots of equipment that we encounter every day, and most of us use computers at school or home, for work and entertainment.

ng presentJul   4 08:48:58 localhost
-sata-root@c/k2 sata/@0:3,\mach_kernel"
ey><string
-sata-root@c/k2
calhost kernel: Got boot device =
cRiscHT/pci@7/IOPCI2PCIBridge/k2-sata-r
ATADeviceNub@0/IOATABlockStorageDriver/
ST3160023AS
led_2@3 Jul   4 08:48:58 localhost

Computers with and without people

Not all computers have a screen and keyboard. Many everyday objects have computers inside them, including mobile phones, DVD players – even cars and washing machines. These are called **embedded computers**. They do a particular task in the piece of equipment they are in. You cannot make them do something else.

If you took apart any computer or piece of computerized equipment, somewhere inside you would find a printed circuit board. This has several computer **chips** and lots of lines printed in metal that form an electrical **circuit**.

The most important chip in a computer is the **microprocessor**. This controls the computer, acting as its "brain". The chips in electronic devices give the instructions that tell the device what to do. The circuit carries an electrical current to move information between the chip and other parts of the equipment. So, if you press a number on your phone, a tiny electrical signal tells the computer chip in the phone that you are dialling a number. When you have finished the number and pressed the dial button, the chip tells the phone to connect to the phone network and pass on the number.

The tiny microprocessors in a mobile phone can handle millions of calculations every second. Ninety percent of all computer chips made are used in consumer electronics items like mobile phones.

This tiny sim card from a mobile phone can store hundreds of phone numbers.

Landmarks in time	**1820s** Charles Babbage designs the Difference Engine	**1830s** Charles Babbage designs the Analytical Engine	**1943-1944** Colossus is built to crack coded German messages in World War II	**1945-1946** ENIAC is built by John Mauchly and J. Presper Eckert

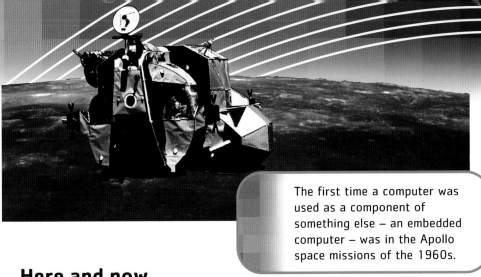

The first time a computer was used as a component of something else – an embedded computer – was in the Apollo space missions of the 1960s.

Here and now

Computers are used in all areas of business, manufacturing, finance, healthcare, and education. We use computers to monitor and predict things that happen around us, such as earthquakes. Computers are helping us to understand our world and the wider Universe.

They also help us to understand ourselves. Computers have made it possible to work out the order of the genes that define human beings. They have also made it possible to predict how new medicines might combat illness.

✕ Make the connection

English mathematician Alan Turing (1912–1954) described something he called a "universal machine" in 1936. This was an ideal computer – a machine that would use numbers and logic to accomplish tasks and carry out any calculation, given the right instructions. Turing later worked on the development of early computers. However, the technology to make the machine he dreamed of did not yet exist.

1952 IBM makes the first mass-produced computer, the Defense Calculator or IBM 701

1964 Douglas Engelbart designs the first system to use icons, windows, and a mouse

1971 Invention of the microprocessor by Ted Hoff

1983 The Apple Lisa is the first personal computer to use a mouse, windows, icons and menus

2002 The tablet PC appears, allowing people to write and draw on a full-size computer by hand with a pen-like stylus

Ideas in action

Computers are all around us and we use them in all areas of our lives, often without even being aware of what they are doing for us.

Chips with everything

A huge amount of computing power is used to make our lives more fun – in mobile phones, games and toys, MP3 players, and even in birthday cards that play a tune.

Pioneer

Toy manufacturer Hasbro launched the first successful mass-market robotic toy, Furby, in 1998. The Furby had sensors that responded to light, movement, sound, and touch, and seemed to react appropriately to play. It would close its eyes and snore in the dark, giggle if tickled, and say it was sad if neglected. In fact, information from the sensors was interpreted by a microprocessor that had instructions telling the Furby how to respond in different situations.

Safety control

Computers control many **safety-critical** systems, in which people's safety depends on the computer working properly. A pilot is helped by lots of computers to keep a plane in the air and comfortably stable. **Sensors** detect how far above the ground the plane is and how fast the wind is blowing. Computers adjust the height and speed of the aircraft as necessary.

Modern hospitals are full of embedded computers running vital equipment. They keep the patient asleep during an operation, run **life-support systems**, and process X-rays and scans. Some even control tiny surgical tools that surgeons use while operating with the help of microscopes and video displays.

A life-support system uses sensors attached to the patient to monitor their condition. As the patient's condition changes, the system adjusts the machines helping the patient's breathing and heartbeat. The life-support system watches the patient all the time and its response is immediate.

Computers in each plane send information by radio to air-traffic control. The computerized air-traffic control systems put all this information together to plan safe flight paths.

Face to face with computers

The point at which people interact with computers is called an interface. The method of using a computer the user interface – should be natural and easy to understand so that the computer is pleasant to use.

Early computers required people to type all their instructions as text. But these instructions could not be in ordinary English; people had to learn exactly the right command for the action they wanted. So, instead of clicking on a picture of a folder to see the files inside, you had to type CAT (for "catalogue") or DIR (for "directory") to see a list of file names on screen.

The idea of using pictures (or icons), menus, and windows on the screen revolutionized the way we use computers. This type of display is called a **graphical user interface**.

>> What is the future?

Consumer electronics, such as personal computers and phones, can do more and more things. We already have phones we can use to search the web, and computers that will show TV programmes. In the future, we might have only one or two items that we use for communications, work, leisure, and maybe other tasks we have not yet thought of. This is called convergence.

The way we interact with computers will rely less and less on typing at a keyboard. Some computers already recognize handwriting and speech, and some can speak to us. Researchers are now working on computers that are controlled by eye movement or even thought.

>< Make the connection

The graphical user interface was first suggested by American Douglas Engelbart in 1962. He developed an early version, and invented the mouse to use with it, in 1964. The first mouse was made of wood; he called it a mouse because the cable connecting it to the computer looked like a long tail. The first commercial computer to use a mouse, windows, menus, and icons was the Apple Lisa, launched in 1983.

Any questions?

Computers have made our lives much better and easier in many ways, but they have also brought new problems.

Some people worry that we depend too much on computers. A major computer failure can stop us using banks, cause traffic jams, or turn off our electricity. Others worry that we are losing some of our skills by relying on computers to do tasks that people used to do.

Many people in the world do not have access to computers. In developing countries, most of the population do not even have phones and radios, let alone the internet or a games console. Even in developed societies, some people have little chance to benefit from computer technologies. As more and more aspects of our lives are managed by computer, people who are left behind will be increasingly disadvantaged.

Wired world

Many of the computers we use do not work alone. More and more equipment is able to share information with other items using networks and communications services.

Back to basics

The computers you use at school or home are probably connected to the internet at least some of the time.

The internet is a huge network of computers all around the world that can share information using telephone lines, radio links, and special cables. Using the internet, we can move information almost instantaneously from one side of the world to the other. We can use it to send email, to search the world wide web, to hold online chats, and to work alongside other people who may be many miles away.

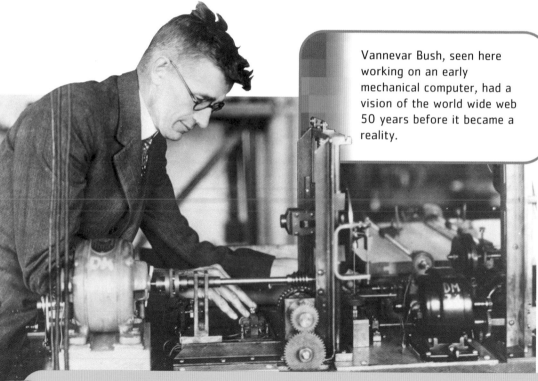

Vannevar Bush, seen here working on an early mechanical computer, had a vision of the world wide web 50 years before it became a reality.

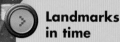

Landmarks in time

1876 Alexander Graham Bell **patents** the telephone

1878 First telephone exchange opened, in New Haven, USA

1956 First transatlantic telephone cable laid between the USA and Europe

1969 Start of ARPANET, the forerunner of the internet, linking four computers in American universities

✕ Make the connection

Before there were any working computers, American Vannevar Bush wrote about a computer system that would allow people to read pages of text on a screen, look at pictures, and jump between linked pages. His work was published in 1945. However, the route from Vannevar Bush's vision to the reality of the world wide web was not straightforward.

The first computer network was called the ARPANET. It was created in 1969 to link the computers of four American universities so that research work could be shared. More university networks joined, and ARPANET became the internet in 1983.

The world wide web was invented in 1990 by Tim Berners-Lee to help researchers work together on projects. He wrote a system of linked pages, all of which could be viewed on the internet. Each page could show either a picture or text, but text and pictures could not be mixed on a single page until 1993, when the Mosaic **web browser** appeared.

As the speed of computers and the internet has increased, the content of web pages has become more complicated. Now, even large photos, complex games, and videos can be included in web pages.

It is not only our desktop and laptop computers that are part of this wired world. Mobile phones, cable television, closed-circuit TV cameras, and many more things share in this connectivity.

Telecommunications – ways of moving or sharing information over distance – has been one of the fastest-growing areas of technology in the last 30 years.

1990 Invention of the world wide web by Englishman Tim Berners-Lee

1993 Mosaic appears, the first web browser that can show both words and pictures on the same web page

1994 *Palo Alto Weekly* in California is the first newspaper to produce an online edition

1995 Online shopping becomes popular with the launch of bookseller Amazon

2001 Filipino president Joseph Estrada removed from power after a demonstration arranged by text message

Here and now

Now, many people have a fast connection to the internet at home. The world wide web provides a wealth of information to anyone who can use a web browser. We can shop, meet new friends, download music, share photos, and watch films. Email and online chat help us to keep in touch with distant (and nearby) friends, with messages taking only a second or two to travel any distance. The internet is now essential for businesses and other large organizations.

It is not only people that use the internet, though. Lots of equipment uses it to send information to the people who need it. Delivery lorries transmit their location and can be tracked on a web page; satellites send information about the weather directly to web pages; a camera in a nursery can use a web page to show parents what their children are doing.

Internet-enabled devices and satellites can be used to track vehicles, objects, and even people or animals. **Global Positioning Systems (GPS)** use a link with a satellite to pinpoint their exact position on Earth. These have been built into phones and many other items. They can even be used to track large animals that are studied in the wild. Elephants can be fitted with collars that have a link to a satellite, for instance.

Many networks still use cables, but others are now wireless. They send information by radio through the air. We can browse the web on a laptop without plugging it in.

Ideas in action

With endless information at our fingertips, new possibilities open up all the time.

Freedom of information

Topics that would have taken weeks to research in libraries can be found quickly and easily on the web. People can find specialized information that they would be unable to get any other way. We can look up medical information when we are ill, compare the details of products we might want to buy, and read online newspapers from around the world to get different angles on news and events. Many major news stories, such as the terrorist attacks on the World Trade Centre in 2001, have been covered live on web news sites as they happened.

It is no longer just newspapers, TV, and radio stations that can publish information – anyone can share their ideas or opinions on the web. Unfortunately, no one checks that the information on the web is accurate or true. We have to use our judgement to decide what we should trust and what we should doubt. There is also a lot of information on the web that many people feel should not be freely available.

>> What is the future?

In the future, more items will use the internet without our intervention. Researchers have developed **prototypes** of fridges that will use the internet to re-order food taken out of them, or to suggest recipes that can be made with the items stored in them.

Smart houses will have many features that can be controlled over the internet. In the USA and Australia, several people have already built houses that use wireless networks and internet connections to control services such as air conditioning, heating and garden sprinklers.

Working together

Project Gutenberg aims to put millions of books, written in the past, on the internet in a form that people can use. All the works of important authors such as Shakespeare, Dickens, Melville, and Tolstoy are already available.

More than 15,000 books have been added since the project started in 1971. It began before the internet even existed, because the project's founder imagined a future in which computers would all be linked and books and other work could be shared. The job of adding new books is done by lots of volunteers around the world. Many hundreds of new books are added to the internet site every month.

There are also several other projects on which experts around the world can collaborate for free, including wikis. A wiki is a website to which anyone can add information or make changes. The idea is that over time a bank of reliable information, added and corrected by experts from all over the world, becomes available to us all. The most famous of these is the wikipedia (www.wikipedia.org), which has articles on half a million topics in English and many in a large number of other languages.

In touch

Some countries try to suppress information and stop people who live there talking to others about sensitive topics. But it is more and more difficult to hide news that is available online, or to stop people communicating when they can use email and text messages to talk to people in other countries. In China, several people were imprisoned for sending emails abroad about the respiratory disease SARS, which struck in 2004. The Chinese authorities were saying the outbreak was not serious, but email messages were showing this was not true.

Blogs, or weblogs, are web pages on which people keep diaries of their activities or thoughts. Salam Pax, known as the "Baghdad blogger", kept an online diary of the lead-up to and progress of the US invasion of Iraq in 2003. His reports of everyday life under Saddam Hussein and then during the war had a worldwide following.

In the immediate aftermath of the tsunami that hit the Indian Ocean in 2004, bloggers passed on news from the scene, helped to co-ordinate relief, posted photos of missing people and survivors, and got news to the outside world hours ahead of the press, TV, and radio.

While internet connections were cut off, bloggers used their mobile phones to send text messages about conditions in areas hit by the tsunami to friends, who then posted the information on blogs.

Search for injured, missing, dead now:

www.hospital.moph.go.th/phuketgpk

www.hospital.moph.go.th/tsunamk

www.disaster.go.th

www.vachira-phuket.go.th

bulaat.phukethospital.com

www.phuketcity.net

Searching For People

In control

The internet can carry information of any kind, including instructions to control equipment. The first object to be controlled over the internet was a toaster in 1990. The power switch was controlled remotely, and later a robotic arm was added to pick up slices of bread and drop them into the toaster.

Real–world playtime

A few games companies have developed online computer games involving people in the real world using mobile phones or GPS systems. In 2005, toy maker Hasbro staged a real-world version of Monopoly, based on GPS systems in London taxis. Players could "buy" property in London and charge

Breakthrough

In 2001, a team of surgeons in New York operated on a woman in France, over 6,000 kilometers (3,700 miles) away. They used cameras and sensors connected to the internet to show them the patient's condition, and controlled robotic surgical tools that carried out the operation. Remote surgery was first tested on a live pig in 1995.

"rent" if the taxi visited it. Other games involve real-world adventures. Players' movements are tracked from the position of their phones and their surroundings can be monitored by cameras and computers.

>> What is the future?

Developments in computers that we can wear or carry around will mean that we can be connected to the internet for more of the time. Mobile phones and PDAs can already be used for email and web browsing, and some toys can access the internet. Soon, digital cameras and PDAs may send our photos and documents to be stored on **web servers**, rather than saving them on a **smart card** or chip in the device itself.

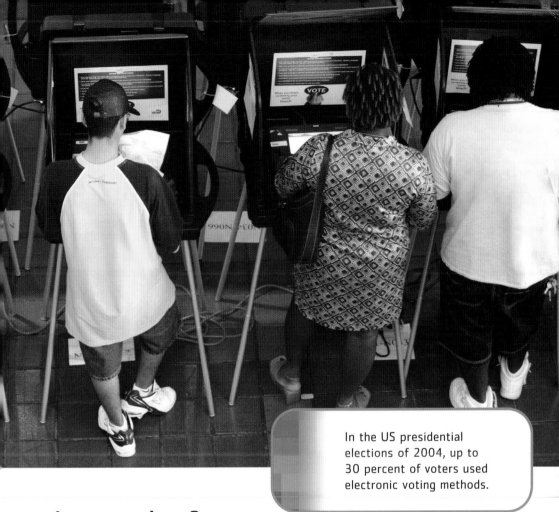

In the US presidential elections of 2004, up to 30 percent of voters used electronic voting methods.

Any questions?

The ease with which information can be shared on the internet alarms many people. In the west, there is a lot of argument about how to protect people, and particularly children, from unpleasant material. Illegal material is difficult to control as it can be stored on computers kept in countries that have no laws about the content of web pages.

Some countries have strict regulations about what people may see on the internet. They have brought in complicated technical systems to restrict what people who live there are able to look at. Some of the information looks harmless to people in other countries. In Saudi Arabia, for example, advertisements for underwear or recipes for alcoholic cocktails are not allowed.

As more of life moves online, people who do not have access to the internet may be left behind. Many of the best deals, from cheap holidays to efficient banking and free information, are only available online. The people who most need them may not have access to them.

Robotics and artificial intelligence

Robots have been common in science fiction since the Czech playwright Karel Čapek produced a play called R.U.R – Rossum's Universal Robots – in 1921.

We still hope for intelligent machines that will carry out the tasks we do not want to do, from cleaning the house to carrying out routine care and nursing tasks. These machines are now getting a lot closer.

Back to basics

A robot is a machine controlled by computer technology that follows instructions to carry out mechanical tasks. Most robots carry out repetitive tasks, or jobs that need great precision and accuracy that are hard for a person to manage. They do not yet think for themselves, though the dream of many people who work in robotics is to create a machine that can think and speak and make decisions for itself, something like a person.

>< Make the connection

Robots began life in fiction. The first actual robots worked in factories, cutting and painting car parts in the 1960s. They looked nothing like the mechanical people familiar from science-fiction movies.

People first began thinking about artifical intelligence (AI) in the 1940s. English mathematician Alan Turing suggested in 1950 that a computer would count as intelligent if it could fool a person having a typed conversation with it into believing that it was human. This is complicated as it needs complete understanding of language. The test, called the Turing Test, is still considered a useful indicator of intelligence in a machine.

Landmarks in time	1921 Czech playwright Karel Čapek produces a play featuring robots	1941-42 Science-fiction writer Isaac Asimov foresees the robotics industry	1943 First artificial neuron (brain cell) created	1950 Turing Test developed by Alan Turing to determine artificial intelligence in a machine

A computer can play chess – it just needs to follow rules and use logic, which computers are good at. The best chess player in the world was beaten by a computer in 1997.

This would be an example of artificial intelligence (AI). Researchers are trying to create artificially intelligent beings (AIs), but progress is slow. For one thing, no one is very sure what intelligence is. Understanding and using language, learning from experience, and understanding what we see are areas that researchers currently think are particularly important.

Here and now

Many factories use robots to build all kinds of products, from large pieces of machinery to tiny computer components.

Robots do many jobs that are dangerous or boring, or that require very precise control. In medicine, tiny robotic tools can be used inside the body, controlled by surgeons. Robots are used to detonate bombs and landmines, to search earthquake wreckage, and to explore dangerous environments like volcanoes and damaged buildings. They can work in conditions that are too dangerous for people, such as places that are very hot or cold, or polluted with poisonous gases or radiation.

1956 George Devol and Joseph Engelberger start the first robot company

1961 The first industrial robot is used at a General Motors car factory in New Jersey, USA

1963 The Rancho robotic arm, controlled by a computer, is designed for use by disabled people

1970 Shakey, the first mobile robot controlled by artificial intelligence, is produced by SRI International

1994 Research on micro-robots that could work together in swarms begins

To make robots more useful, scientists are using AI in their development. Experts are trying to make robots that can "see", that can understand spoken instructions, or that can actually learn new things.

An **expert system** is a computer system that has a huge collection of information about a complicated subject, such as medicine or engineering. It can search its bank of information and make suggestions, comparisons, or decisions, often more quickly and thoroughly than a human expert. Expert systems are used in many fields, but they cannot copy the imagination, vision, or intuition of a human expert.

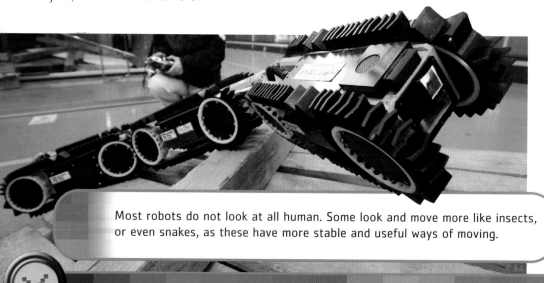

Most robots do not look at all human. Some look and move more like insects, or even snakes, as these have more stable and useful ways of moving.

⟩⟨ Make the connection

The idea for neural computer networks came from the way the human brain works. Your brain has up to 100 billion nerve cells, called **neurons**. Each one is connected to about 10,000 other neurons and can pass signals to any of them.

The idea for an artificial **neural network** first appeared in 1943, when scientists trying to understand the working of the brain made an artificial neuron called a perceptron. As computer technology developed in the 1950s, it became possible to build a simple neural network.

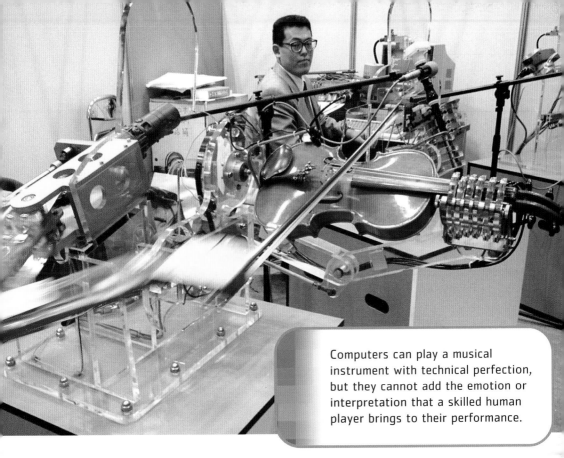

Computers can play a musical instrument with technical perfection, but they cannot add the emotion or interpretation that a skilled human player brings to their performance.

Ideas in action

It is very difficult to make computers or robots that can think, as we do not really understand ourselves how we think and learn.

Learning to learn

It might be possible for a robot or computer to use the same methods as the human brain to learn new information and change its behaviour. Early robots just followed a set of instructions, but the latest robots can learn simple things. A small roving robot can learn a route around a room or maze, remembering where there are objects or corners. It uses this information to take a direct route, avoiding bumps, on its next trip.

Computers that learn use a type of system called a neural network.

Neural networks are good at complicated jobs like recognizing patterns. This is vital in making a computer that can see. A traditional computer would check one possibility after another, but the neural network tries out lots of possible patterns at the same time. If a particular match is successful, it is more likely to be used again. Next time the same problem is encountered, the previously successful match will be tried first. This is how a computer system learns.

On its own

A robot that can act intelligently on its own would be useful in many different situations. At present, robots are often used to gather information and carry out physical tasks in environments people cannot work in. Many of these robots contain advanced computers; some use neural networks and can learn to some extent.

Robots work on their own at tasks such as space exploration, mining deep underground, or investigating the deep seabed and the inside of volcanoes. A robotic lander on any planet further away than Mars is too far away to take instructions from a computer on Earth. Even though communications travel at the speed of light, the distances are so great

The **probe** Huygens landed on Titan, a moon of Jupiter, in 2005. It took photographs and sent information back to Earth.

that messages take too long to go backwards and forwards. Robotic landers that can look after themselves and make simple decisions will be essential for space exploration beyond the solar system.

Team robots

Robots that work without people do not always work alone. Swarms of small robots working together have been used for some tasks. In 2000, robotics researcher Rush Robinett developed a swarm of tiny robots that communicate with each other constantly to look for people lost in avalanches and skiing accidents. The same swarming techniques can be used to find earthquake survivors. The robots can be the size of a large insect.

This makes it easy for them to run through small spaces, and light enough to cross fragile structures. Scientists are finding lots of uses for swarms of robots that will act together, communicating with radio waves and sharing what they have learned.

One of us

Rodney Brooks, director of the AI laboratory at the Massachusetts Institute of Technology, has investigated the nature of intelligence and how it can be built into a computer or robot. With a team of researchers, he is building Cog, the most advanced human-like robot. Cog should be able to learn from its experiences and eventually develop the intelligence of a two-year-old baby.

» What is the future?

A robot the size of an insect is small, but they could be about to get even smaller. Scientists are now working on **nanotechnology**. This involves extremely small machines and computer systems. They hope we may soon have miniature robots that can be put inside the body to carry out operations and repair damage to tissues and organs. A tiny robot might patrol your blood vessels, removing built-up fat, or may follow a blood vessel into the heart to investigate and make repairs.

Just like us

It is very easy for us to walk, dance, or play football – but very hard for a robot. When you move, your brain makes lots of very quick calculations about your surroundings, your balance, and what you can see. Copying these tasks in a robot is very challenging.

Robotics experts in Japan have built robots that can belly-dance (by copying the way an eel moves); play football; dance to hip-hop tunes; and even sing and dance at the same time. These are not just for fun. Teaching a robot to play football involves overcoming difficult problems in robotics. A footballer has to balance on one foot while kicking, watch a moving ball, be able to tell where it will go, and judge the best way to kick it – all without falling over. One dancing robot has been taught traditional Japanese dances that are dying out. It is hoped that the robot will offer a way of preserving this part of Japanese culture for the future.

A dancing robot does not need to learn the moves. It must match the way it moves to the music, balance and be able to correct itself if it starts to topple.

» What is the future?

At the moment, most robots look nothing like a person. But scientists are working on soft-bodied robots that could have skin and hair. Robots might also have artificial muscle fibres and be powered by glucose (a sugar), just like our bodies. Possible uses suggested for human-like robots with some intelligence include routine nursing and care tasks.

Any questions?

There are many more questions than answers in the field of artificial intelligence. People do not agree on the nature of human intelligence. We do not fully understand how we learn, see, or develop languages. A computer can do better than a human at tasks that require logic or skills, but it is not able to recognize a flower in a crowded scene or understand a joke.

There are several limitations to our knowledge about robotics and artificial intelligence.

There are also many **ethical** and moral questions that must be answered. Philosophers working in this area discuss questions such as:

- Would an intelligent, thinking machine be conscious? If so, does that mean it is alive?
- If a machine is conscious or alive, should it have rights? Should there be limits to what we make it do?
- Would it be right to allow a thinking machine to have feelings?

Imaging and modelling

Computer images are all around us. These range from computer games to weather forecasts, from **ultrasound** scans of unborn babies to the latest blockbuster movies, where most special effects are now created by computers.

Back to basics

Computer images are a type of model. A model is a copy or **simulation** of something in the real world, a copy of something that could exist, or even of something completely imaginary.

✕ Make the connection

Early computers only used text. In 1963, American Ivan Sutherland developed the first computer-graphics program as part of his PhD thesis. Called Sketchpad, it was an "object-oriented" graphics program. This means that elements of a drawing can be moved, changed, or magnified with no loss of quality and without affecting other parts of the drawing. Sketchpad revolutionized the way computers could be used.

Once computers could display pictures, the detail and accuracy improved quickly as people found new uses for imaging and modelling. Instead of just showing pictures drawn by a person on the computer, computers became capable of making pictures from information. If a computer is given all the dimensions and shapes of a new building, it can make a picture of it, show it from different angles, and even allow us to "walk through" a model of the building.

Landmarks in time	1952 A. S. Douglas writes the first computer game, *tic-tac-toe*, played against the EDSAC computer,	as part of his PhD thesis at Cambridge University, England	1962 Steve Russell writes *Spacewar*, the first commercial computer game	1963 Ivan Sutherland produces Sketchpad, the first object-oriented computer-graphics program

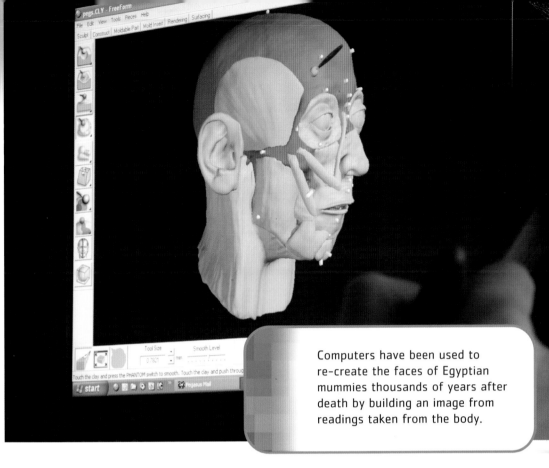

Computers have been used to re-create the faces of Egyptian mummies thousands of years after death by building an image from readings taken from the body.

Some kinds of model show us information in the form of words and numbers. A spreadsheet can be a type of model. It can show how fast a disease might spread, or how much a business could expect to make from a new product. Others kinds of model show pictures or moving images.

A computer can turn information from a scan made with ultrasound or **infrared** into a picture or map of a body, place, or object. Medical images are made in this way. It is much easier to understand a visual image like this, than a list of words or numbers.

Models and images are commonly used for entertainment, in computer games and in movie special effects.

| **1978** Creation of the first **virtual-reality** system, the Aspen Movie Map, at MIT. It crudely re-created | Aspen, Colorado, in summer and in winter. | **1978** VisiCalc, the first spreadsheet program, is produced by Dan Bricklin and Bob Frankston | **1995** *Toy Story* from Disney/Pixar is the first feature film created entirely on computer | **2001** *Final Fantasy* from Columbia Pictures is the first **photo-real** movie created entirely on computers |

Here and now

Computer models are used to try out designs for new buildings, vehicles, products, and medicines. We can model populations, the spread of disease, and even the expansion of the Universe or the first moments of its existence.

Modelling is used to predict what will happen in situations that are difficult, expensive, or dangerous to try out. For example, a space mission is modelled on computer to make sure the spacecraft will behave suitably in different possible situations. We also use models, called simulators, to help people learn how to pilot planes and ships. New pilots can learn the skills they need in a way that will not endanger real passengers.

You may be used to playing computer games. Some, like *Age of Empires* and *The Sims*, let you create a whole society in a model on the computer. This is both a graphic model and an information model. You can see your buildings and move your characters around, and you can achieve success or failure, for example, depending on how you trade in your imaginary economy.

Ideas in action

Computer modelling and imaging are amongst the most exciting and entertaining uses of computers. We see examples almost every day in one form or another.

Animated films like *Shrek* are made completely on computer. The characters are computer models with programmed movements.

» What is the future?

Film-makers want to make more realistic computer-based animations. The film *Final Fantasy* (2001) was the first to try to look like a real-action film while being made entirely on computers. When the techniques have been perfected, film studios could make new films featuring dead actors. They would create their stars' performances on computers using models developed from all the films they made in life.

Dead film stars like Marilyn Monroe could be "brought back to life" on computer screens to make new movies.

Computer film stars

The stars of some movies do not exist outside a computer. Some films combine real and computer-generated characters, and others are made entirely on computers.

In real-action films, actors sometimes have to pretend there is a monster, alien, or some other creature on the set. Characters like these are created on computers and added to the film later.

Often, many similar imaginary characters are needed, such as an army of alien warriors or a swarm of insects. To make them each behave differently, animators produce a set of varied actions, responses, and characteristics.

Each individual is created by combining elements chosen from this set and follows their programming to create the action. Because the characters behave differently, there is plenty of variety in the scene and it looks like a group of individuals. But no one has to work out and animate the actions of each one – the computer does that.

Animated characters in movies like *Shrek* are designed as **wire-frame** models. A computer program then moves them, works out the effects of lighting and shadows, and changes their surface textures (clothing, hair, fur) as they move. It also makes sure the environment is suitably changed - for example, by making the characters leave footprints or press down grass.

Computer-generated images

The Disney/Pixar movie *Toy Story* (1995) was the first animated feature film to be made entirely on computer using computer-generated images (CGI). After all the characters, action, sets, and lighting were designed (all done on computer), each frame of the film was "rendered" or created from all the information. Pixar used over 100 Sun workstations and took between 2 and 13 hours to render each frame. There are 144,000 frames in the 77-minute long movie, so that is around 90 years of computing time in total!

Animated characters like Sulley and Mike in the Disney/Pixar movie *Monsters, Inc.* (2001) are first developed as so-called wire-frame models.

Computers are being used to model and plan the evacuation of the Italian city of Naples, which lies in the shadow of the volcano Vesuvius. Vesuvius erupts several times a century and there have been many serious eruptions.

Looking ahead

Computer models are often used to predict future events or conditions. The weather forecast is probably the most familiar. Computers look at past weather sequences for patterns that repeat in the information. Then they work out what is likely to happen next by comparing these patterns with current weather conditions.

Computers are also used to predict more dramatic events. Around the world, earthquake and volcanic activity is monitored all the time.

From comparing current readings with past patterns, computers can sometimes predict an earthquake or eruption.

When a disease threatens to turn into an epidemic, such as the outbreak of bird flu in Asia in 2004, scientists use computers to model the way it may spread and the number of cases they may have to deal with. This helps people to plan the healthcare that is needed and to make sure that there is enough medicine.

Playtime

People's wish to play computer games full of action and exciting images has helped drive the development of faster computers with better graphics.

The first games were simple and only lasted a few minutes. Many involved shooting aliens or moving around a maze collecting rewards and avoiding hazards. Games have become increasingly complex. Most are now simulations or models of some kind, from car racing to empire building. They include huge amounts of information. Some games come on several CD-ROMs.

One CD-ROM can hold information equivalent to about 100 million words – about 10,000 times as many as in this book!

One of the latest developments in computer games is virtual reality (VR). This is a complete simulated environment in which players are immersed. VR can include all-round graphics, sound, and motion. A special kind of glove, wired up to the computer, can be used to give instructions in a VR environment. It can also give feedback to the player, showing how objects feel, for example.

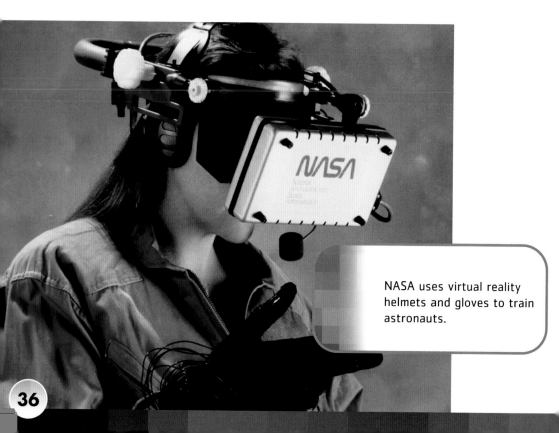

NASA uses virtual reality helmets and gloves to train astronauts.

>> **What is the future?**

The future of computer games is likely to include more use of VR. Games will have increasingly realistic graphics and will provide more sensory involvement for players. People playing VR games want to be completely immersed in the imaginary environment. One possibility is complete VR suits, or rooms which hold a VR environment. At the moment, VR goggles change the view shown as a player turns their head. In a VR room, the scene is projected onto all four walls.

Any questions?

Computer games have been blamed for many social problems. Some people believe that children and teenagers who spend too long playing computer games do not develop social skills, or may suffer health risks from spending too much time using a screen and mouse or games controller. There are concerns that games with a frightening, aggressive, violent, or highly competitive content may be psychologically or emotionally damaging. If VR games are very violent, complete immersion in the experience could be especially damaging.

If computers can generate perfect actors, will real actors lose out? Just as people in the 1970s and 1980s worried that their jobs in offices and factories might be taken over by computers, so now actors feel their jobs may be threatened.

Cyber threats

Computer security has become a serious worry, especially for organizations that keep very important information on computers. Threats to computer systems include **hackers**, **viruses, worms**, and even terrorist attacks.

Back to basics

Anyone who has a computer has to take care to protect it against attacks that could cost them valuable information or could stop their computer working. A computer connected to the internet is at risk in several ways.

Viruses can be spread from one computer to another when information is moved between them, either on CDs, disks, and memory sticks, or by email and web pages. Viruses attach themselves to other programs. They are not able to move between computers on their own.

A worm is a program that can spread itself over the internet or another network, moving independently. It copies itself onto any connected, unprotected computer. Worms often spread by email, sending themselves to all the contacts in an email address book.

A **Trojan** is a program that looks as though it may be useful but includes a part that does damage or sends out information from the infected computer to someone else.

Spyware is a small program that sends information from the infected computer to somewhere else. It can be installed on a computer without the owner's knowledge if they do not have good enough protection. Spyware can track and pass on passwords, personal details, and other valuable or sensitive information.

A hacker is someone who breaks into a computer without permission. They may steal valuable information, make changes, or delete information. Hackers are a threat to businesses and large organizations such as banks, governments, and national security systems.

Landmarks in time	**1960s-1970s Phone phreaking** emerges as the first form of hacking	**1982** Harmless virus affecting Apple computers released by Richard Skrenta	**1983** First malicious virus is produced as a "proof of concept" by Fred Cohen	**1988** Robert Morris releases the first effective internet worm

Viruses may do anything from displaying an annoying message to deleting information or stopping a computer from working at all.

1990-1992 Great Hacker War, in which rival gangs of hackers, the Masters of Deception and the Legion of Doom, compete to hack into major computer

systems, causing the US Secret Service to crack down on hacking

2000 Liberty Crack, the first Trojan to infect hand-held computers, is released in Sweden.

2004 Cabir is the first computer worm to spread over the mobile phone network

Here and now

If you have an email account, you are probably used to receiving **spam**. This is email sent out to large numbers of people, often advertising products or web pages. Spam is annoying, but for most people is no more dangerous than that. Some spam, though, has an attached file with a virus, or a link to a web page that will infect your computer if you follow it. Many people protect their computers with anti-virus software, spam filters (to remove the spam as it arrives), **firewalls**, and software to protect against spyware.

Individuals are rarely the targets of hackers, who are more likely to try to steal or change information held by large corporations and government departments.

To protect our own information, we use passwords and secret information that is **encoded** before travelling over the internet, so that it cannot be stolen in transit. To try to guard against international terrorism and other crime, security organizations scan email and other communications.

✕ Make the connection

The first harmful computer virus was created in 1983 by Fred Cohen, an American student studying for a PhD. He created it as part of an experiment in computer security. People had suggested that a program that copied itself and damaged computers would be possible. Science fiction had mentioned computer viruses since the mid–1970s. Cohen proved they could exist. He added his virus to a graphics program and it infected other areas of the same computer within an hour. People were so alarmed by Cohen's virus that further research was banned.

A harmless virus called Elk Cloner was released in 1982 by Rich Skrenta (shown here as an adult) when he was just 15 years old. It affected Apple computers and displayed a poem every 50th time the computer was started.

Ideas in action

Threats come from virus programmers, hackers, and people who use the internet for illegal activities.

So many computers are now online that the internet has become the main route for spreading viruses and worms.

Catching viruses

A computer virus attaches itself to a computer program. When the program is run, the virus may either run itself, doing something disruptive, or copy itself into other programs. Most viruses have separate copying and damaging phases. This lets them copy themselves undetected for a while and then begin to do damage to the infected computer.

In recent years, viruses and worms have caused havoc as they have spread around the world in a matter of hours. The I LOVE YOU virus cost US$7,000 million worldwide in 2000; Code Red copied itself 250,000 times in the first nine hours after it was released in 2001; Melissa (1999) was the fastest-spreading virus ever seen.

Sabotage and theft

Hackers break through computer security systems to steal, change, or delete valuable information. Some hackers take great pride in their skill. They hack into the systems that should be the most secure, such as military and government computers, and just leave a message to show that they have been there. Other hackers do real damage.

In the film *War Games* (1983), a young boy hacks into a computer and nearly starts World War III as the US military computers try to launch a counter-attack against the non-existent threat he has set up.

Pioneer

The most notorious hacker in the USA is Kevin Mitnick, though others have caused more damage. Kevin was first arrested for phone phreaking committed in 1981. However, he has been imprisoned for computer crimes several times and was once held in solitary confinement for eight months because prison authorities thought he could start a nuclear war using only the prison's pay phone. He agreed to take counselling for his computer addiction, but reoffended. He was banned from using the internet for a year after his release from prison in 2002.

Viruses are no longer restricted to computers. They are appearing on other consumer electronics, such as PDAs and mobile phones. As we rely more and more on electronic devices and telecommunications, more areas of our lives will be threatened by attacks from hackers, spies, and virus writers.

More of our equipment uses computers and networks than ever before. Hackers and viruses could even attack the computer systems in our cars or other items that we do not think of as being computers.

"Phishing" is a way of tricking people into revealing information that will then make them vulnerable.

A common phishing practice is to send emails to people that appear to be from their banks asking them to verify their security passwords. Victims follow a link to a website that looks like their bank's site and give the information. The thieves then take money from their victims' bank accounts.

Identity theft is a growing threat. Hackers steal information that identifies people and sell these identities on to criminals. Criminals pretend to be someone else as a way of carrying out crimes and getting away with them. The victims of identity theft can end up owing money, being unable to get work or credit, and being accused of crimes they have not committed.

>> What is the future?

So far there has not been a large-scale cyber terrorist attack, though terrorists routinely use the internet to communicate and co-ordinate real-world attacks. Governments and other large organizations worry that an attack on a computer system could cause huge damage. It could be limited to financial loss, but if terrorists brought down a nuclear power station or air-traffic control system, for example, this could cause loss of life, too.

Staying safe

Everyone who uses a computer will be used to having to give a secret password to use their own account or settings, either on the computer or on a website. A password keeps you safe only as long as no one else knows it. If it is easy to guess, or someone steals it, the information you thought was safe becomes vulnerable.

Passwords and credit-card details are **encrypted** to stop them being stolen from a computer or intercepted as they are sent over the internet. Encryption means that the details are turned into a code. There are very complicated ways of doing this so that the codes are practically unbreakable.

The internet has made it easy for criminals to get in touch with one another. Many countries have seen an alarming rise in criminal information distributed on the internet. Websites promoting racial and religious hatred and describing how to carry out illegal activities mean that more people than ever have easy access to information they could use to harm others. Children have sometimes been lured into meeting people they have chatted to online and have then been abducted or harmed. Protecting people from threats like this is a challenge to us all.

The first cyber terrorist attack was carried out by an offshoot of the Sri Lankan separatist group the Tamil Tigers against Sri Lankan embassies in Europe, North America, and Asia.

Any questions?

The most pressing questions about computer threats concern personal freedoms and our right to privacy. How can these be balanced against the need for national and personal safety?

The most secure methods of encryption are illegal. This is because governments and police authorities in some countries do not want there to be any information that they cannot look at if they are suspicious. They also scan all communications looking for clues that might alert them to planned or past crimes and terrorist attacks. The international organization Echelon uses computers to scan up to 3 billion telecommunications every day, including phone calls, web downloads, faxes, and email messages.

Many people object that their right to privacy has been sacrificed in the hope that we may interrupt or prevent criminal activity. A balance between personal freedom and international security is difficult to establish.

Now that the internet is so widely used, it has become easy for people to spy on other people by looking at their email or checking which websites they have visited. Some employers look at their employees' email and web histories to check that they only use the computer for their work. Some parents check their children's computers to make sure they are not visiting unsuitable websites, or having email and chat conversations with unsuitable people.

Faster and smaller

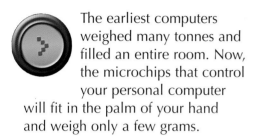

The earliest computers weighed many tonnes and filled an entire room. Now, the microchips that control your personal computer will fit in the palm of your hand and weigh only a few grams.

Back to basics

The speed at which a computer works is called its processing speed. A modern desktop computer can carry out many millions of instructions per second. Computer developers are constantly trying to make their computers faster so that we can do more with them.

A hand-held PDA can contain fast, powerful computer chips but can still be very small. This is because it does not need the other parts found in a desktop computer, such as a CD ROM/DVD drive.

Early computers were programmed by making connections with wires. This took a very long time and had to be carried out by skilled workers.

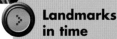

Landmarks in time

1906 Invention of the vacuum tube or valve, making digital electronic computers possible

1947 Invention of the transistor by William Shockley, John Bardeen, and Walter Brattain

1954 Silicon transistor introduced by Texas Instruments

1965 Gordon Moore forecasts that the speed of computers will double every 18 months – known as Moore's Law

✂ Make the connection

Instead of integrated circuits and chips, the first computers used heavy **valves** of the kind used in old radios. Colossus, the code-breaking computer developed at Bletchley Park in 1943, had 1,500 valves. These failed frequently and had to be replaced immediately.

The invention of the transistor in 1947 meant that valves could be replaced by something much smaller. The invention of the printed circuit board, which miniaturized whole electric circuits, made even smaller computers possible. Finally, the invention of the microprocessor made personal computers possible.

How it works

Modern computer chips hold very complex circuits **etched** into thin pieces of **silicon** wafer. Each chip holds several patterns of circuits in layers. These make a 3-D block of etched circuitry. The lines of the circuits are too small to see with the naked eye yet they contain millions of interconnected devices. They can only be made by computerized equipment.

Here and now

Many people believe we are approaching the limits of size and speed for the technologies we have. Chips have been made to work more quickly by making them smaller, so that electrical charges have a shorter distance to travel along the circuitry. The distances in some circuits are now measured in numbers of atoms.

1971 Invention of the microprocessor by Ted Hoff

1985 David Deutsch publishes an outline for a universal **quantum computer**

1988 Invention of the optical chip, which uses light instead of electricity as a power source

1994 Peter Shor devises the first calculation a quantum computer could do

Computer manufacturers are looking at ways of reducing the time it takes for information to travel between chips and the rest of the computer. One way forward may be to use **optical fibres** and lasers to replace wiring. Information will then move at the speed of light.

Computers have been made faster using a technique called parallel processing. Instead of a single processor working on one task at a time, two or more processors split the work between them. Supercomputers use large numbers of fast processors working together like this.

The fastest supercomputer at the moment is being developed by IBM. Called BlueGene/L, it can already perform over 130,000 billion calculations a second (or 130 "**teraflops**"). The most powerful desktop computers perform less than one teraflop. When finished, BlueGene/L will have 65,536 processors and work at a speed of 360 teraflops.

Desktop and laptop computers could also be smaller if they used power more efficiently, so the power supply and motor could be smaller. Personal electronics like MP3 players use solid-state storage devices instead of disks. This means that the information is stored electronically on a computer chip. It is smaller and quicker to read and write to than a disk, but cannot yet hold as much information.

>> What is the future?

Researchers are developing a miniature camera and computer worn as a brooch or necklace that records all that happens during a day. If you lost something, you could replay the record of the day and see where you put it. Also being developed are jackets which can receive email, and paper wristwatches that take the time from radio signals and reset themselves if the wearer goes into a different time zone. Soon, we may be wearing and carrying much more computer technology.

Ideas in action

As computers become smaller, faster, and more versatile, we are able to use them in different ways. Tiny computers can be incorporated into clothing and jewellery, or used in systems that are themselves very small, such as medical implants.

Wearable computing

Wearable computers are computers built into clothing or jewellery. "Smart" accessories could respond to changes in our bodies and remind us to take medicines, for example.

One development is glasses that will project an image in front of the wearer's eyes. A system for astronauts will show images and instructions inside the visors of their spacesuits. This would help them with tasks on space walks on the International Space Station.

This jacket combines mobile telephony, an MP3 player, and a keyboard on the sleeve.

Worn on the inside

Miniaturized computers can be used inside the body as well as worn outside.

A **retinal** implant could be put into the eye of a blind person to restore some level of vision. It has a group of microscopic light-sensitive cells. The light picked up by these cells is converted into an electrical impulse and passed to the surrounding tissue. This copies the way the cells in the retina of an undamaged eye send information to the brain as an electrical impulse.

The microchip that controls the process is about one millimetre (0.04 inch) across. It will be several years before retinal implants are ready for human patients, as more testing and development is needed to perfect them.

A cochlear implant is fitted by surgeons into a deaf person's ear to enable them to hear again. It converts sounds to electrical impulses to send from the ear to the brain.

Biological computers

Our brains are the most powerful computers we know of, and they work using chemistry rather than electronics. Some scientists think chemistry may be the way forward for artificial computers, too.

We are more likely to think of DNA as the building blocks of life than of computers. It is the material genes are made of. It carries the instructions that describe our bodies in a chemical code. Because DNA stores and works with complex information, it may be possible to use it for computing tasks. Scientists have already found a way to carry out calculations using DNA and hope one day to use DNA in a computer chip.

✕ Make the connection

In 1994, Leonard Adleman suggested that DNA could be used to solve mathematical problems. He argued that DNA in our cells acts a bit like a computer hard disk as it stores all the information about us in a coded sequence. DNA's code is made from sequences of proteins. Adleman used the protein sequences to stand for things in a problem. He then started a chemical reaction to produce lots of possible answers.

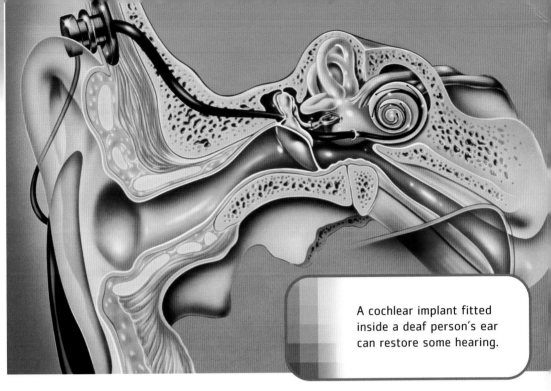

A cochlear implant fitted inside a deaf person's ear can restore some hearing.

DNA computers are still a long way off, but if we can make them, they will give us fast, tiny computers that can tackle problems of the type neural networks are good at – looking for patterns and processing many possibilities at the same time. About half a kilogram (one pound) of DNA could store more information than all the electronic computers in the world today.

Nanotechnology

Microtechnology is built at the level of microns; a micron is very small, just one thousandth of a millimetre. Scientists are already making microtechnologies and are exploring the possibilities of nanotechnology. Nanotechnology is a thousand times smaller – millionths of a millimetre.

At this level, we are working with individual atoms and molecules. We can already make some nanotech components. This is usually achieved by using chemical reactions rather than traditional micro-engineering methods with physical tools. In 2004, for example, scientists found a way to grow nanocrystals inside bacteria. The nanocrystals can be used in tiny electronic devices.

One possible use for nanotechnology is to make nanobots. These are extremely small robots that can build very small components (including more of themselves). They could have a large number of uses, from manufacturing to breaking down pollutants in soil or water.

Quantum computing

While nanotechnology offers a way of making computers and machines much smaller, quantum computing could offer a way of making them much faster. Although, we cannot yet build a practical, working quantum computer, features of quantum mechanics (the behaviour of particles smaller than atoms) could be used to carry out calculations and move information. Quantum particles do not follow the traditional laws of physics, so their behaviour opens up huge possibilities if we can harness it.

Any questions?

The questions we must ask about future developments in making smaller and faster computers are "Are they possible?" and "Do we want them?" It seems likely that we are approaching the limits of size and speed using the technologies we currently have. Although wearable computers and computerized implants use very small computer components, these are on the level of microtechnology rather than nanotechnology.

Some people worry that nanotechnology holds a great threat to our future. If we can build devices that make copies of themselves, they could quickly get out of hand. An error in programming could lead to things going wrong. For example, a nanobot that is supposed to clean up pollution might start removing a substance vital to our existence instead, or pollute all the world's seas in a matter of days.

Quantum computing is further off. We have become good at observing quantum effects; now we need to develop new ways of working with and controlling these effects for quantum computing to become a real possibility. It might seem that this is a long way off, but 100 years ago we did not have a single computer. Progress can be surprisingly rapid.

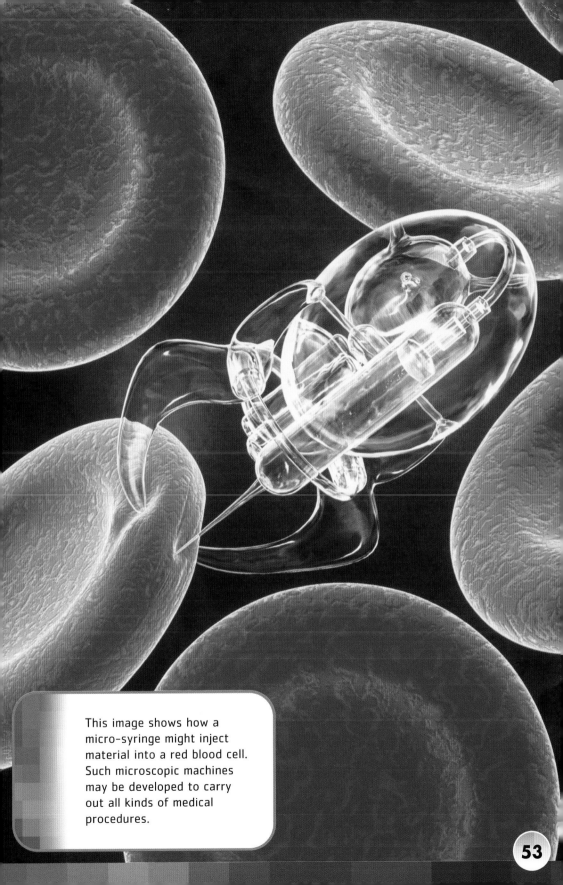

This image shows how a micro-syringe might inject material into a red blood cell. Such microscopic machines may be developed to carry out all kinds of medical procedures.

Glossary

blog online diary or journal kept by one person, sometimes contributions from others

chip see microchip

circuit wiring and components making up a pathway along which electricity travels

embedded computer computer that is a part of another piece of equipment

encoded turned into code

encrypt disguise information by turning it into a code

etch engrave by cutting away part of the surface with acid or other chemical

ethical relating to whether things are morally right or wrong

expert system computer system that consults a large database of expert knowledge in order to make decisions or predictions

firewall software or device to restrict access to and from the Internet on a computer

Global Positioning Systems (GPS) device that refers to satellites to determine its geographic position on Earth

graphical user interface way of using the computer that uses graphics such as windows, menus, icons, and a pointer moved by a mouse

hacker person who breaks into computers illegally to take, change, or destroy information

infrared energy beyond red light in the electromagnetic spectrum

life-support system system of computers and machinery that helps to keep very sick hospital patients alive

microchip very small silicon wafer etched with circuitry, including the microprocessor that carries out calculations or control

microprocessor computer component that carries out calculations or control

nanotechnology very small scale engineering

neural network electronic system that works like the human brain

neuron single brain cell

optical fibre extremely thin, hollow glass fibre used to carry data

patent legal recognition of ownership of an idea or invention

PDA personal digital assistant: hand-held computer

phone-phreaking breaking into phone networks illeagally to make phone calls without paying for them

photo-real realistic, like a photograph

printed circuit see printed circuit board

probe robot or other device used to investigate a hard-to-reach location

prototype early, trial version of something

quantum computer new type of computer that works by using the properties of atomsor even smaller particles to represent bits of information

retina inside back surface of the eye lined with light-sensing cells

safety critical system in which safety is vitally important

semiconductor material that can conduct electricity in certain conditions but not as well as most metals do.

sensor device used to determine changes in conditions such as temperature or light intensity

silicon chemical element that has some of the properties of metal, but is not a true metal

simulation something which imitates the appearance or nature of something else

smart card plastic card with an embedded computer chip that holds information about someone or something

spam unwanted email sent to many people at once

spyware software that spies on a person's computer use and sends information to a distant computer

supercomputer very fast, powerful computer with many processors

telecommunications electronic systems for moving information long distances

teraflop measure of the speed of computers: one teraflop processes a million million instructions a second

transistor device used in computers to switch electrical current on and off

Trojan computer program that is presented as one thing but actually does something different and usually harmful

ultrasound sound waves outside the range people can hear, used to produce scans by recording echoes

valve glass tube enclosing a vacuum used in early computers to switch electrical current on and off

virtual reality realistic computer-generated environment

virus computer program that spreads by changing another program and then copying itself

web browser computer application used for displaying and working with pages on the world wide web

web server computer on which web pages are stored for people to look at using the world wide web

weblog see blog

wire-frame outline model of a figure that looks as though it is made of thin wires

worm computer program that can spread itself from one computer to another, usually using the Internet

Further resources

How Computers Work, Ron White, Timothy Edward Downs, Que, 2003

How Things Work: An Illustrated Encyclopedia of the Amazing World of Technology, Chris Oxlade, Lorenz Books, 2002

Riotous Robots, Mike Goldsmith, Scholastic, 2004

Tomorrow's Science: Artificial Intelligence, Anne Rooney, Chrysalis, 2003

Tomorrow's Science: Internet Technologies, Anne Rooney, Chrysalis, 2003

Index